COLORING BOOKS
FOR TEENS
RELAXATION

Dolphins & More

Preview of Coloring Pages

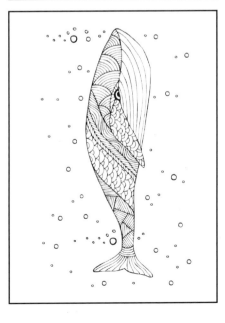

Preview of Coloring Pages

Did You Enjoy Our Coloring Book?

We Want To Hear About It!

Help spread the word about our coloring books! The best way to spread the word is through reviews. We know how busy you are, especially with all of that coloring, but we would appreciate it!

Visit our website at www.arttherapycoloring.com

Over 200 Art Therapy Coloring Books

See our collection of over 200 Art Therapy Coloring Books for Adults, Men, Women, Seniors, Teens, Kids, Boys, and Girls.

Coloring Books For Girls

Art Therapy Coloring Books

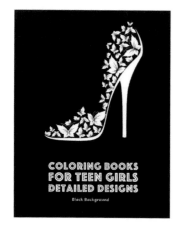

COLORING BOOKS
FOR TEEN GIRLS
DETAILED DESIGNS
Black Background

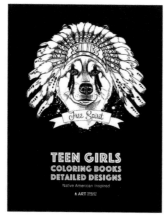

TEEN GIRLS
COLORING BOOKS
DETAILED DESIGNS
Native American Inspired

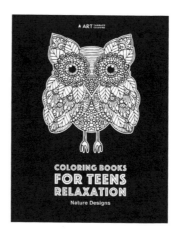

COLORING BOOKS
FOR TEENS
RELAXATION
Nature Designs

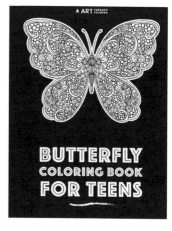

BUTTERFLY
COLORING BOOK
FOR TEENS

COLORING BOOKS
FOR TEEN GIRLS VOL 2
DETAILED DESIGNS

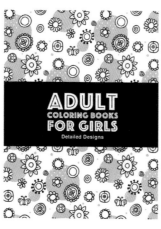

ADULT
COLORING BOOKS
FOR GIRLS
Detailed Designs

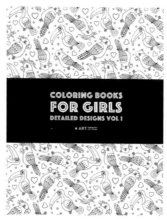

COLORING BOOKS
FOR GIRLS
DETAILED DESIGNS VOL 1

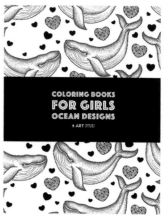

COLORING BOOKS
FOR GIRLS
OCEAN DESIGNS

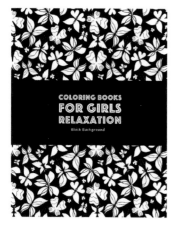

COLORING BOOKS
FOR GIRLS
RELAXATION
Black Background

COLORING BOOKS
FOR OLDER KIDS
GEOMETRIC DESIGNS

HEART
COLORING BOOK
FOR KIDS

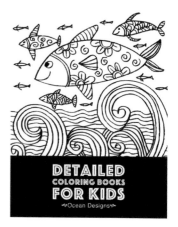

DETAILED
COLORING BOOKS
FOR KIDS
Ocean Designs

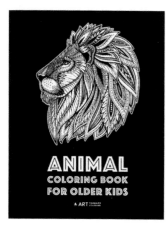

ANIMAL
COLORING BOOK
FOR OLDER KIDS

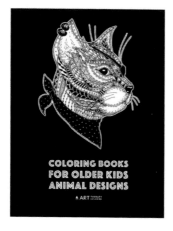

COLORING BOOKS
FOR OLDER KIDS
ANIMAL DESIGNS

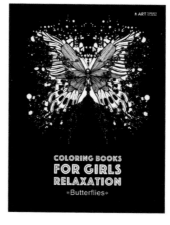

COLORING BOOKS
FOR GIRLS
RELAXATION
Butterflies

BUTTERFLY
COLORING BOOK
FOR KIDS
Detailed Designs

Coloring Books For Kids

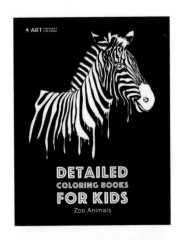

DETAILED COLORING BOOKS **FOR KIDS**
Zoo Animals

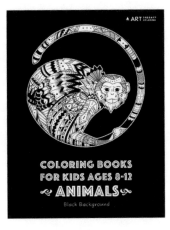

COLORING BOOKS FOR KIDS AGES 8-12 **ANIMALS**
Black Background

DETAILED COLORING BOOKS **FOR KIDS**

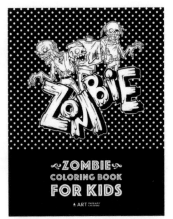

ZOMBIE COLORING BOOK **FOR KIDS**

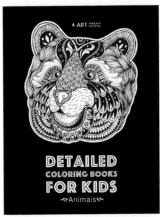

DETAILED COLORING BOOKS **FOR KIDS**
Animals

DETAILED COLORING BOOKS **FOR KIDS**
Elephants

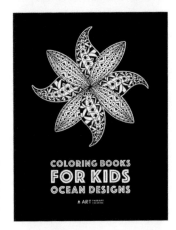

COLORING BOOKS **FOR KIDS** OCEAN DESIGNS

MANDALA COLORING BOOK **FOR KIDS**
Black Background

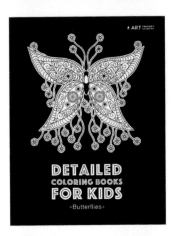

DETAILED COLORING BOOKS **FOR KIDS**
Butterflies

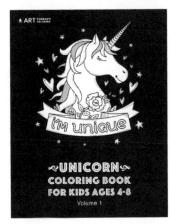

UNICORN COLORING BOOK FOR KIDS AGES 4-8
Volume 1

UNICORN COLORING BOOK FOR KIDS AGES 4-8
Volume 2

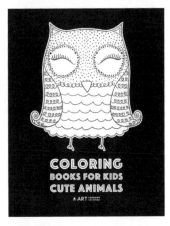

COLORING BOOKS FOR KIDS CUTE ANIMALS

KIDS MANDALA COLORING BOOK

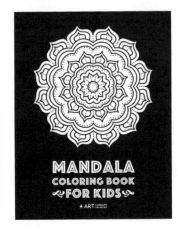

MANDALA COLORING BOOK **FOR KIDS**

SHARK COLORING BOOK

DINOSAUR COLORING BOOK

Coloring Books For Boys

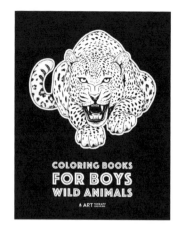

COLORING BOOKS
FOR BOYS
WILD ANIMALS

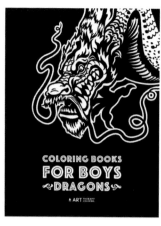

COLORING BOOKS
FOR BOYS
~ DRAGONS ~

COLORING BOOKS
FOR BOYS
ANIMAL DESIGNS

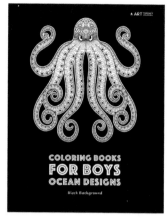

COLORING BOOKS
FOR BOYS
OCEAN DESIGNS
Black Background

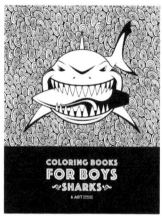

COLORING BOOKS
FOR BOYS
~ SHARKS ~

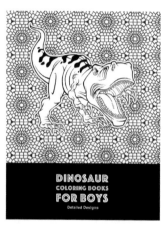

DINOSAUR
COLORING BOOKS
FOR BOYS
Detailed Designs

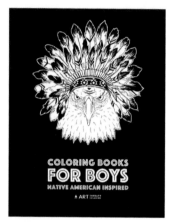

COLORING BOOKS
FOR BOYS
NATIVE AMERICAN INSPIRED

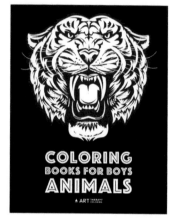

COLORING
BOOKS FOR BOYS
ANIMALS

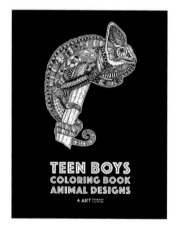

TEEN BOYS
COLORING BOOK
ANIMAL DESIGNS

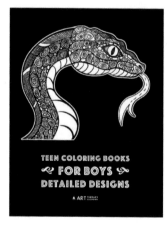

TEEN COLORING BOOKS
~ **FOR BOYS** ~
DETAILED DESIGNS

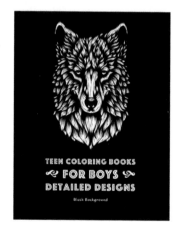

TEEN COLORING BOOKS
~ **FOR BOYS** ~
DETAILED DESIGNS
Black Background

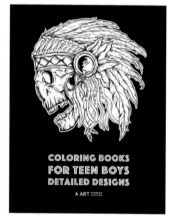

COLORING BOOKS
FOR TEEN BOYS
DETAILED DESIGNS

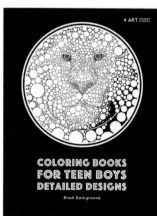

COLORING BOOKS
FOR TEEN BOYS
DETAILED DESIGNS
Black Background

ADULT
COLORING BOOKS
FOR KIDS
Geometric Designs

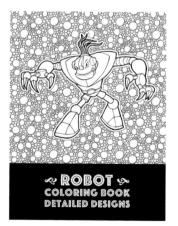

~ **ROBOT** ~
COLORING BOOK
DETAILED DESIGNS

DETAILED
COLORING BOOKS
FOR KIDS
Geometric Designs

Coloring Books For Teens

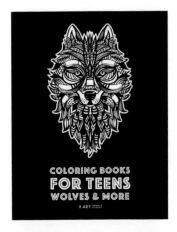

COLORING BOOKS
FOR TEENS
WOLVES & MORE

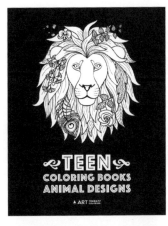

~TEEN~
COLORING BOOKS
ANIMAL DESIGNS

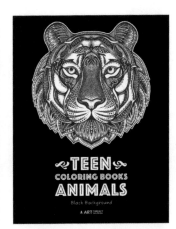

~TEEN~
COLORING BOOKS
ANIMALS
Black Background

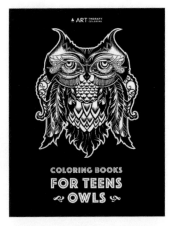

COLORING BOOKS
FOR TEENS
~ OWLS ~

~TEEN~
INSPIRATIONAL
COLORING BOOKS

~TEEN~
COLORING BOOKS
ANIMAL DESIGNS
Black Background

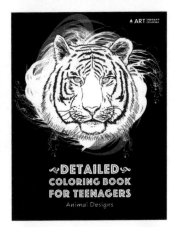

~DETAILED~
COLORING BOOK
FOR TEENAGERS
Animal Designs

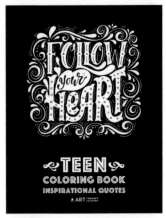

~TEEN~
COLORING BOOK
INSPIRATIONAL QUOTES

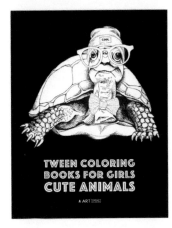

TWEEN COLORING
BOOKS FOR GIRLS
CUTE ANIMALS

ADULT COLORING BOOKS
~ FOR TEENS ~
Animal Designs

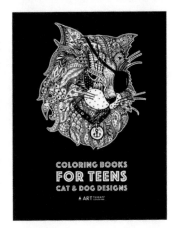

COLORING BOOKS
FOR TEENS
CAT & DOG DESIGNS

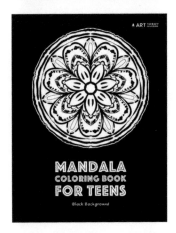

MANDALA
COLORING BOOK
FOR TEENS
Black Background

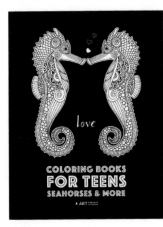

COLORING BOOKS
FOR TEENS
SEAHORSES & MORE

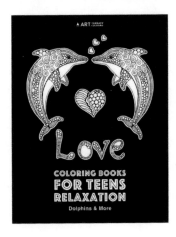

COLORING BOOKS
FOR TEENS
RELAXATION
Dolphins & More

~TEENS~
COLORING BOOK
OCEAN THEME

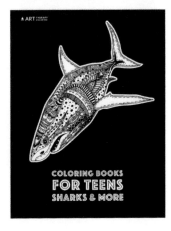

COLORING BOOKS
FOR TEENS
SHARKS & MORE

Coloring Books For Teens

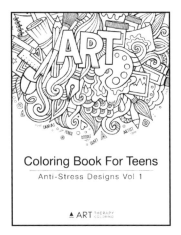

Coloring Book For Teens
Anti-Stress Designs Vol 1

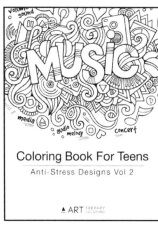

Coloring Book For Teens
Anti-Stress Designs Vol 2

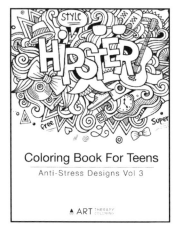

Coloring Book For Teens
Anti-Stress Designs Vol 3

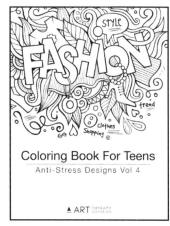

Coloring Book For Teens
Anti-Stress Designs Vol 4

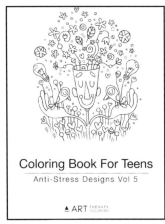

Coloring Book For Teens
Anti-Stress Designs Vol 5

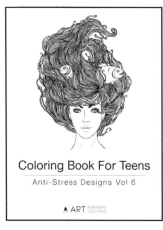

Coloring Book For Teens
Anti-Stress Designs Vol 6

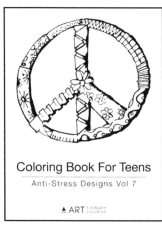

Coloring Book For Teens
Anti-Stress Designs Vol 7

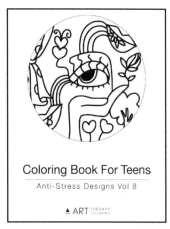

Coloring Book For Teens
Anti-Stress Designs Vol 8

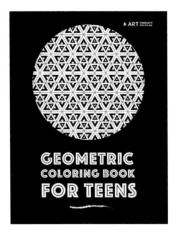

GEOMETRIC COLORING BOOK FOR TEENS

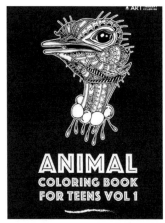

ANIMAL COLORING BOOK FOR TEENS VOL 1

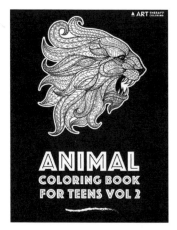

ANIMAL COLORING BOOK FOR TEENS VOL 2

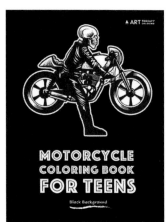

MOTORCYCLE COLORING BOOK FOR TEENS
Black Background

COLORING BOOKS FOR TEENS OCEAN DESIGNS

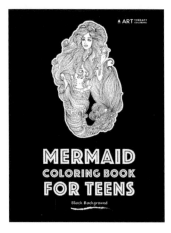

MERMAID COLORING BOOK FOR TEENS
Black Background

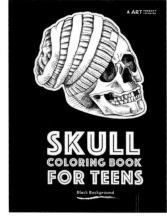

SKULL COLORING BOOK FOR TEENS
Black Background

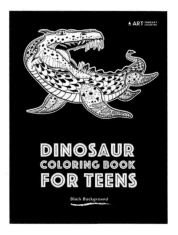

DINOSAUR COLORING BOOK FOR TEENS
Black Background

Coloring Books For Adults

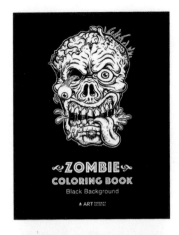

ZOMBIE
COLORING BOOK
Black Background

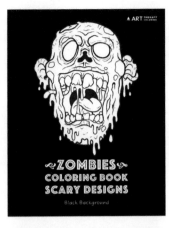

ZOMBIES
COLORING BOOK
SCARY DESIGNS
Black Background

DRAGON
COLORING BOOK

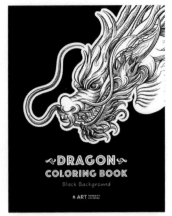

DRAGON
COLORING BOOK
Black Background

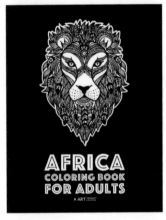

AFRICA
COLORING BOOK
FOR ADULTS

LION
COLORING BOOK
FOR ADULTS

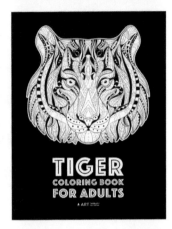

TIGER
COLORING BOOK
FOR ADULTS

WILD ANIMALS
COLORING BOOK
ZENDOODLE DESIGNS

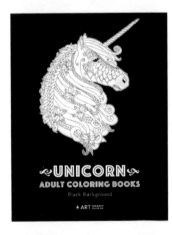

UNICORN
ADULT COLORING BOOKS
Black Background

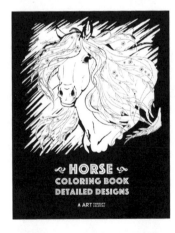

HORSE
COLORING BOOK
DETAILED DESIGNS

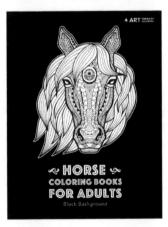

HORSE
COLORING BOOKS
FOR ADULTS
Black Background

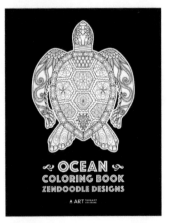

OCEAN
COLORING BOOK
ZENDOODLE DESIGNS

WOLF
COLORING BOOK
FOR ADULTS

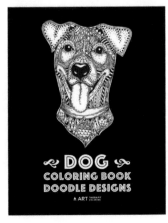

DOG
COLORING BOOK
DOODLE DESIGNS

CUTE ANIMAL
COLORING BOOK

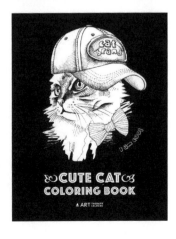

CUTE CAT
COLORING BOOK

Coloring Books For Adults

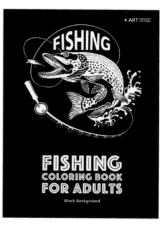

Coloring Books For Adults

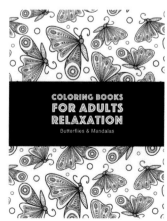

Coloring Books For Seniors

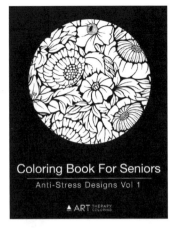

Coloring Book For Seniors
Anti-Stress Designs Vol 1

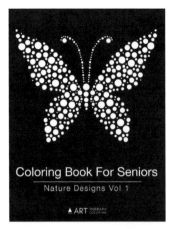

Coloring Book For Seniors
Nature Designs Vol 1

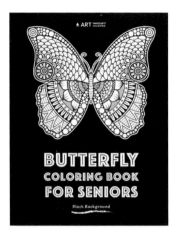

BUTTERFLY
COLORING BOOK
FOR SENIORS
Black Background

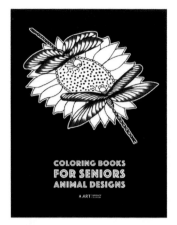

COLORING BOOKS
FOR SENIORS
ANIMAL DESIGNS

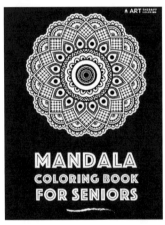

MANDALA
COLORING BOOK
FOR SENIORS

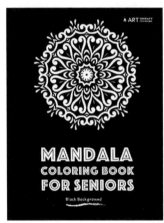

MANDALA
COLORING BOOK
FOR SENIORS
Black Background

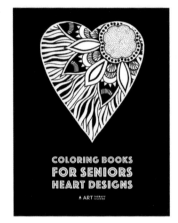

COLORING BOOKS
FOR SENIORS
HEART DESIGNS

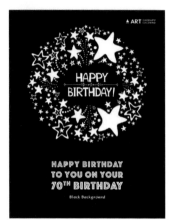

HAPPY BIRTHDAY
TO YOU ON YOUR
70TH BIRTHDAY
Black Background

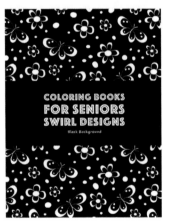

COLORING BOOKS
FOR SENIORS
SWIRL DESIGNS
Black Background

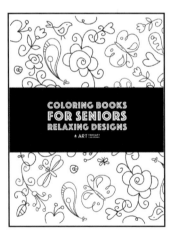

COLORING BOOKS
FOR SENIORS
RELAXING DESIGNS

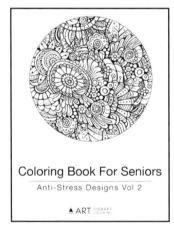

Coloring Book For Seniors
Anti-Stress Designs Vol 2

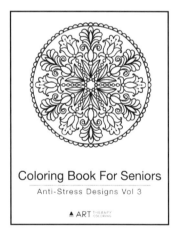

Coloring Book For Seniors
Anti-Stress Designs Vol 3

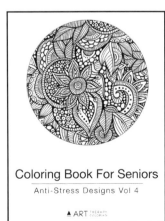

Coloring Book For Seniors
Anti-Stress Designs Vol 4

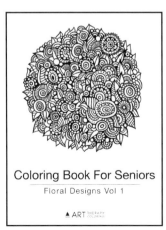

Coloring Book For Seniors
Floral Designs Vol 1

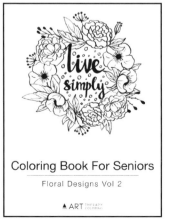

Coloring Book For Seniors
Floral Designs Vol 2

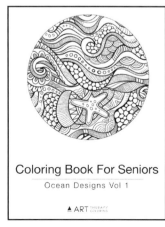

Coloring Book For Seniors
Ocean Designs Vol 1

Coloring Books For Men

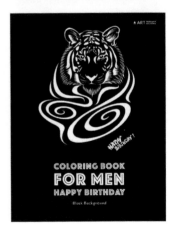

Coloring Books For Special Occasions

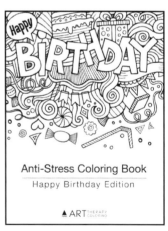

Coloring Books For Teens Relaxation
Dolphins & More

Published by:
Art Therapy Coloring
El Dorado Hills, California
www.arttherapycoloring.com

Shutterstock Images

ISBN: 978-1-64126-095-4

CPSIA information can be obtained at www.ICGtesting.com
Printed in the USA
BVIW10 334190520
0024B/435